Pancakes

Delicious family recipes

igloo

igloo

Published in 2011

by Igloo Books Ltd

Cottage Farm

Sywell

NN6 0BJ

www.igloo-books.com

Food photography and recipe development: Stockfood, The Food Image Agency

Front and back cover images © Stockfood, The Food Image Agency

L006 1210

10 9 8 7 6 5 4 3 2 1

ISBN: 978 0 85734 595 0

Front cover photograph © Stockfood/Antje Plewinski

Printed and manufactured in China

641.8153

CONTENTS

SWEET

SAVOURY

CHILDREN'S

SWEET
PANCAKES

PANCAKES WITH STRAWBERRY JAM AND BERRIES

Serves: 4
Prep and cook time: 20 minutes

Method

Put the flour in a bowl, add the sugar, salt, beaten eggs and milk and beat well to make a smooth batter.

Heat a little of the butter in a 20 cm / 8" frying pan and pour in 2 - 3 tablespoons of the batter. Tilt the pan to spread the mixture evenly and cook for about 1 minute.

Flip the pancake over with a palette knife and cook for another minute or until golden brown. Put the pancake on a plate to cool. Repeat with the rest of the batter.

To serve, spread a little strawberry jam on each pancake. Roll up the pancakes, dust them with icing sugar, decorate with fresh berries and serve.

Ingredients:

150 g / 6 oz plain (all purpose) flour
1 tbsp sugar
pinch of salt
2 eggs, beaten
250 ml / 8.7 fl. oz milk
2 tbsp butter

To serve:

strawberry jam
icing (confectioners') sugar
mixed berries

BANANA AND
PECAN PANCAKES
WITH ORANGE SYRUP

Serves: 4
Prep and cook time: 30 minutes

Ingredients:

For the batter:

125 g / 4.4 oz plain (all purpose) flour, sifted
1 tsp baking powder
pinch of salt
1 tbsp sugar
1 egg, beaten
250 ml / 8.7 fl. oz milk
1 tbsp melted butter
2 bananas, thinly sliced
60 g / 2.1 oz pecan nuts, finely chopped
vegetable oil, for frying

For the orange syrup:

100 g / 3.5 oz sugar
juice and zest of 2 oranges
2 tbsp water

To serve:

vanilla ice-cream

Method

Put the flour in a bowl and add the baking powder, salt, sugar, egg, milk and melted butter. Beat well to make a smooth batter and stir in the banana slices and chopped pecans.

Heat a little oil in a frying pan. Using a large tablespoon of batter, make several small, thick pancakes. Allow space for the mixture to spread. Cook for 1 - 2 minutes or until bubbles start to rise to the top, then turn the pancakes over with a palette knife and cook for another minute or until golden brown. Continue with the rest of the batter.

To make the syrup, put the sugar in a small pan with the orange juice and zest and the water. Bring to the boil and simmer for 5 minutes.

Serve the pancakes with vanilla ice-cream drizzled with orange syrup.

9

SOUR CREAM PANCAKES
WITH PLUM JAM AND CREAM

Serves: 4
Prep and cook time: 30 minutes

Method

Mix the egg yolks with the sour cream, sugar, flour and salt and beat well to make a smooth batter.

Beat the egg whites in a clean bowl until they form soft peaks, then fold gently into the batter mixture.

Heat a little of the butter in a frying pan and drop in small spoonfuls of the batter, allowing space for it to spread a little. Cook the pancakes for 1 minute on each side or until golden brown. Repeat until the mixture is used up, adding more butter as needed.

To serve, layer the pancakes with the whipped cream and plum jam and sprinkle with cinnamon and icing sugar.

Ingredients:

For the batter:

3 eggs, separated
250 ml / 8.7 fl. oz sour cream
2 tbsp sugar
150 g / 5.3 oz flour
pinch of salt
2 tbsp butter, for frying

For the filling:

250 ml / 8.7 fl. oz double cream, lightly whipped
6 tbsp plum jam (jelly)
cinnamon powder
icing (confectioners') sugar

BAKED CRÊPES
WITH VANILLA
CREAM

Serves: 4
Prep and cook time: 1 hour

Ingredients:

For the batter:

125 g / 4.4 oz plain (all purpose) flour, sifted
pinch of salt
1 tbsp sugar
1 egg, beaten
250 ml / 8.7 fl. oz milk
50 g / 2 tbsp butter, for frying

For the vanilla cream:

500 ml / 16.5 fl. oz milk
1 vanilla pod, split lengthways
100 g / 3.5 oz sugar
3 egg yolks, beaten
3 tsp cornflour
100 g / 3.5 oz raisins

Method

Put the flour in a bowl, add the salt, sugar, beaten egg and milk, and mix to make a smooth batter. Set the mixture aside for 20 minutes.

To make the vanilla cream, heat the milk in a small pan with the vanilla pod and sugar. Add the egg yolks and stir over a very gentle heat until the mixture thickens, taking care not to let it boil. Mix the cornflour with a little water and stir into the vanilla cream. Heat gently for 2 minutes, then stir in the raisins. Once cooled, remove the vanilla pod.

Heat the oven to 200°C (180°C fan) 400°F, gas 6.

Heat a little bit of the butter in a frying pan and pour in 2 tablespoons of the batter. Tilt the pan to spread the mixture evenly and cook for 1 minute. Turn the crêpe over with a palette knife, cook for another minute or until it is golden brown, then transfer it to a plate. Repeat with the rest of the batter.

Butter an ovenproof dish and pour in a little of the vanilla cream. Spread 2 tablespoons of vanilla cream on to each crêpe. Roll them up and place them in the dish. Pour over the remaining vanilla cream.

Bake for 10 minutes or until the vanilla cream is bubbling. Sprinkle with icing sugar and serve hot.

MINI-PANCAKE
TOWER WITH
LEMON CREAM

Makes: 12 pancakes
Prep and cook time: 2 hours 30 minutes

Ingredients:

For the batter:

1 sachet easyblend yeast
1 tsp sugar
75 g / 2.6 oz plain (all purpose) flour, sifted
75 g / 2.6 oz buckwheat flour, sifted
1 egg, separated
250 ml / 8.7 fl. oz milk
1 tsp salt
vegetable oil, for frying

For the lemon cream:

1 tbsp icing (confectioners') sugar
2 egg yolks
200 g / 7 oz mascarpone
juice of 2 lemons

To garnish:

zest of 2 lemons
icing (confectioners') sugar, for dusting

Method

Put the yeast, sugar and two kinds of flour into a bowl with the egg yolk, milk and salt and beat well to make a smooth batter. Cover with a damp tea towel and put in a warm place to rise for about 2 hours.

To make the lemon cream, beat the icing sugar with the egg yolks until light and fluffy. Beat the mascarpone with the lemon juice, then gradually fold in the sugar and egg yolk mixture.

To finish the pancakes, whisk the egg white until soft peaks appear. Fold it into the batter mixture. Heat a little oil in a frying pan and drop on spoonfuls of the batter to make pancakes about 6 cm / 2 ½" in diameter. Cook the pancakes for 2 minutes or until bubbles appear on the surface, then turn them over with a palette knife and cook for 2 more minutes or until golden brown.

To assemble the pancake towers, spread a pancake thickly with lemon cream, add another pancake and more lemon cream, and continue until the towers are 3 - 4 pancakes high.

CHOCOLATE CHERRY PANCAKES
WITH BANANAS

Serves: 4
Prep and cook time: 40 minutes

Ingredients:

For the batter:

125 g / 4.4 oz plain (all purpose) flour, sifted
2 tbsp cocoa powder, sifted
pinch of salt
1 tbsp sugar
1 egg, beaten
250 ml / 8.7 fl. oz milk
vegetable oil, for frying

For the chocolate sauce:

100 g / 3.5 oz dark chocolate, chopped
1 tbsp butter
2 tbsp double cream

For the filling:

4 tbsp black cherry jam (jelly)
3 bananas
fresh cherries
vanilla ice-cream

Method

Put the flour into a bowl, add the cocoa powder, salt, sugar, egg and milk and beat together to make a smooth batter.

Heat a little oil in a 20 cm / 8" frying pan. Pour in 2 large spoonfuls of batter, tilting the pan so that it spreads evenly. Cook the pancake for 1 minute, then turn it over with a palette knife and cook for another minute, or until golden brown. Repeat with the rest of the batter.

To make the chocolate sauce, melt the chocolate in a bowl over a pan of simmering water. Beat in the butter and cream, then remove from the heat.

Spread black cherry jam on the pancakes and add slices of banana. Roll up the pancakes, drizzle with chocolate sauce and serve with fresh cherries and vanilla ice-cream.

APPLE PANCAKES
WITH CINNAMON SUGAR

Serves: 4
Prep and cook time: 40 minutes

Ingredients:

For the batter:

125 g / 4.4 oz plain (all purpose) flour, sifted
2 tbsp sugar
pinch of salt
2 eggs, beaten
200 ml / 7 fl. oz milk

For the filling:

4 tbsp butter
2 large cooking apples, peeled, cored and sliced
2 tsp cinnamon powder
4 tsp icing (confectioners') sugar

Method

Put the flour in a bowl, add the sugar, salt, eggs and milk and beat well to make a smooth batter.

Melt 1 tablespoon of butter in a 20 cm / 8" frying pan and gently cook a quarter of the apple slices for 5 minutes, or until they start to brown. Carefully pour over a quarter of the pancake batter and cook for 2 minutes. Turn the pancake over with a palette knife and cook for another 2 minutes until golden brown.

Repeat with the rest of the apples and batter mixture, stacking the pancakes between sheets of kitchen parchment. Cover the pancakes with a clean tea towel to keep warm.

Sprinkle cinnamon and icing sugar over the pancakes and serve warm.

SAVOURY
PANCAKES

POTATO PANCAKES
WITH SALMON
AND HORSERADISH

Serves: 4
Prep and cook time: 45 minutes

Ingredients:

For the batter:

2 large potatoes,
peeled and chopped
2 tbsp butter
85 g / 3 oz plain (all
purpose) flour, sifted
2 eggs, beaten
100 ml / 3.5 fl. oz milk
vegetable oil, for frying

To serve:

1 tbsp creamed
horseradish
1 tbsp double cream
8 slices smoked salmon
2 tbsp caviar or salmon
roe (optional)
chives

Method

Boil the potatoes in a large pan of water for 15 minutes or until tender. Drain and mash thoroughly with the butter.

Mix the flour with the eggs and milk and beat in the cooled mashed potato to make a smooth, thick batter. Season with salt and pepper.

Heat a little of the oil in a frying pan and drop in spoonfuls of the batter, allowing it to spread evenly.

Cook the pancakes for 2 minutes, then turn them over with a palette knife and cook for another 2 minutes or until golden brown. Repeat with the rest of the batter, adding more oil if necessary.

Mix the horseradish with the cream and season with salt and pepper.

Serve the pancakes with the smoked salmon and horseradish cream, topped with caviar (optional) and chive stalks.

CRISPY PEKING DUCK PANCAKES

Serves: 4
Prep and cook time: 2 hours 30 minutes

Ingredients:

2.5 kg / 5.5 lbs prepared duck
25 g / 1 oz fresh ginger, peeled and grated
2 tbsp salt
2 tbsp five-spice powder

For the batter:

140 g / 5 oz plain (all purpose) flour
½ tsp salt
125 ml / 4.2 fl. oz boiling water
2 tbsp sesame oil

To serve:

4 spring onions, shredded
hoi sin sauce, or plum sauce

Method

Heat the oven to 170°C (150°C fan) 340°F, gas 5.

Run the grated ginger around the cavity of the duck and rub inside and out with the salt. Rub the five-spice powder into the skin of the duck. Put the duck on a rack in a deep roasting pan and roast in the oven for 1 ½ hours, draining the fat every half an hour. Turn the oven up to 200°C (180°C fan) 400°F, gas 6 and cook for another 20 minutes, or until the skin is brown and crispy.

To make the pancakes, put the flour and half a teaspoon of salt into a bowl and stir in the boiling water. When the dough is cool enough to handle, knead it on a floured board for 10 minutes until it is smooth, then cover with a clean tea towel and leave for 30 minutes.

Knead the dough again for 5 minutes, then roll it into a sausage shape and cut it into about 12 pieces. Dip each piece in a little sesame oil and roll into a thin circle about 10 cm / 4" in diameter.

Brush a frying pan with the remaining sesame oil and heat. Gently fry the pancakes in batches until they start to colour. Stack them between sheets of kitchen parchment and cover with a clean tea towel to keep warm.

Once the duck has finished cooking, leave the meat to rest for 10 minutes before shredding and serving.

25

RED PEPPER, GOATS' CHEESE AND HAM CRÊPES

Serves: 4
Cooking time: 1 hour 15 minutes

Method

Heat the oven to 160°C (140°C fan) 320°F, gas 3.

Remove the seeds from the red peppers. Slice the peppers into strips. Season the strips with salt, sprinkle with sugar and bake for 30 minutes.

To make the crêpes, put the flour in a bowl and add the salt, beaten egg and milk. Beat the mixture well to make a smooth batter.

Heat the oil in a 20 cm / 8" frying pan, pour in 1 - 2 large spoonfuls of batter and tilt the pan so the mixture spreads thinly. Cook for 1 minute, then turn the crêpe over with a palette knife. Cook for another minute or until golden brown. Repeat with the rest of the batter, adding more oil if necessary.

Remove the peppers from the oven and turn the heat up to 200°C (180°C fan) 400°F, gas 6.

Fold the crêpes into quarters and place on a baking sheet. Put half a slice of Serrano ham onto each one, top with a slice of goats' cheese and season with salt and pepper.

Bake in the oven for 8 minutes or until the goats' cheese starts to melt. Scatter the baked red peppers over the top and serve.

Ingredients:

For the batter:

125 g / 4.4 oz plain (all purpose) flour, sifted
pinch of salt
1 egg, beaten
300 ml / 10.5 fl. oz milk
vegetable oil, for frying

For the topping:

200 g / 7 oz goats' cheese, sliced
6 slices Serrano ham
2 red peppers
pinch of salt
2 tsp sugar

PANCAKE PARCELS
WITH CHILLI

Serves: 4 (or 8 - 10 as a starter)
Prep and cook time: 1 hour

Ingredients:

For the batter:

125 g / 4.4 oz plain (all purpose) flour, sifted
pinch of salt
1 egg, beaten
300 ml / 10.5 fl. oz milk
vegetable oil, for frying

For the filling:

2 tbsp oil
1 onion, finely chopped
1 clove garlic, chopped
1 red chilli, finely chopped
1 tsp ground cumin
1 tsp ground cinnamon
1 tsp ground coriander
400 g / 1 lb minced beef
400 g / 14 oz tinned tomatoes
400 g / 14 oz tinned kidney beans

To serve:

12 sprigs rosemary

Method

Put the flour in a bowl, add the salt, beaten egg and milk and beat well to make a smooth batter.

For the filling, heat the oil in a large pan and gently fry the onion for a few minutes until softened. Add the garlic and chilli. Stir in the cumin, cinnamon and ground coriander, then add the beef and stir over a high heat for 2 minutes or until the meat is browned.

Add the tomatoes, turn down the heat and simmer gently for 30 minutes.

To make the pancakes, heat a tablespoon of oil in a 20 cm / 8" frying pan, pour in a large spoonful of batter and tilt the pan so the mixture spreads thinly and evenly. Cook for 1 minute, then turn the pancake over with a palette knife. Cook for another minute or until golden brown. Repeat with the rest of the batter, adding more oil if necessary.

Drain and rinse the kidney beans, stir them into the meat mixture and gently heat through.

To serve, put a spoonful of the chilli meat mixture on to each pancake, draw up the edges to form a parcel and secure with a sprig of rosemary.

PANCAKES WITH AUBERGINE AND FETA CHEESE

Serves: 4
Cooking time: 45 minutes

Method

Put the flour into a mixing bowl, add the salt, milk and egg and beat together to make a smooth batter.

Heat 2 teaspoons of oil in a 20 cm / 8" frying pan. Pour in 1 - 2 spoonfuls of batter and immediately tilt the pan so the mixture spreads evenly.

Cook for 1 minute, turn the pancake over with a palette knife and cook for another minute or until golden brown. Repeat with the rest of the batter.

Rinse the aubergine slices under running water and pat dry with kitchen paper. Heat the olive oil in a wide pan and gently fry the aubergine slices in batches until lightly browned on each side. Keep the cooked slices warm.

Dress the shredded lettuce with the lemon juice.

Fold each pancake in half, place two slices of aubergine, two slices feta and some lettuce in the middle, season with a little oregano, salt and pepper and roll up to form a cone. Secure each cone with a chive stalk and garnish with fresh mint and olives.

Ingredients:

For the batter:

125 g / 4.4 oz plain (all purpose) flour, sifted
pinch of salt
250 ml / 8.7 fl. oz milk
1 egg, beaten
vegetable oil, for frying

For the filling:

1 large aubergine (eggplant), cut into ½ cm slices
3 tbsp olive oil
½ iceberg lettuce, shredded
juice of 1 lemon
200 g / 7 oz feta cheese, sliced
2 tsp dried oregano
12 chive stalks
fresh mint, to garnish
black olives, to garnish

BUCKWHEAT PANCAKES WITH CHEESE AND LEEKS

Serves: 4
Prep and cook time: 1 hour

Ingredients:

For the batter:

60 g / 2 oz buckwheat flour
60 g / 2 oz plain (all purpose) flour
1 egg, beaten
125 ml / 4.4 fl. oz milk
125 ml / 4.4 fl. oz water
½ tsp salt
vegetable oil, for frying

For the filling:

1 tbsp olive oil
1 clove garlic, chopped
100 g / 3.5 oz bacon, diced
2 leeks, sliced
75 g / 2.6 oz Gruyère, grated
1 tbsp crème fraiche

Method

Put the flour into a bowl and add the beaten egg, milk, water and salt. Beat well to make a smooth batter. Leave the mixture to stand for 30 minutes.

Heat a little oil in a 20 cm / 8" pan and pour in a large spoonful of the batter, tilting the pan so it spreads evenly. Cook the pancake for a minute, then turn it over with a palette knife and cook until lightly browned. Repeat with the rest of the batter.

For the filling, heat the oil in a wide pan and cook the garlic, bacon and leeks for about 10 minutes, stirring frequently. Season with salt and pepper, remove from the heat and stir in the cheese and crème fraiche.

Place a little of the filling on to each pancake and fold into triangles.

CHILDREN'S
PANCAKES

BANOFFEE PANCAKES

Makes: 12
Cooking time: 1 hour

Method

Place the unopened tin of condensed milk in a pan of water. Bring the water to the boil and simmer for 40 minutes, topping up the water if necessary. This will make the banoffee sauce.

To make the pancakes, put the flour, salt, sugar, baking powder, melted butter, milk and beaten eggs into a bowl, and beat together until smooth.

Heat 2 teaspoons of oil in a frying pan and drop in a tablespoon of the pancake batter. Allow to cook for 2 minutes or until bubbles start to appear on the top. Turn the pancake over with a palette knife and cook until golden brown. Repeat with the rest of the batter.

Whip the cream with the icing sugar, carefully open the tin of condensed milk and slice the bananas.

Layer the pancakes with the whipped cream and sliced bananas, and drizzle with banoffee sauce.

Ingredients:

For the batter:

250 g / 8.8 oz plain (all purpose) flour, sifted
½ tsp salt
2 tsp sugar
2 tsp baking powder
2 tbsp melted butter
300 ml / 10.5 fl. oz milk
2 eggs, beaten
vegetable oil, for frying

For the filling:

400 ml / 14 fl. oz tin condensed milk
300 ml / 10.5 fl. oz whipping cream
2 tbsp icing (confectioners') sugar
4 bananas

CHOCOLATE CHIP PANCAKES

Makes: 12
Cooking time: 45 minutes

Method

Put the flour into a bowl, add the cocoa powder, baking powder, sugar, salt and milk, and beat to make a smooth batter. Set the batter aside to rest for 20 minutes.

Meanwhile, melt the chopped chocolate in a bowl over a pan of simmering water. Once melted, remove the chocolate from the heat, beat in the cream and the melted butter and keep warm.

Heat the maple syrup in a small pan, stir in the strawberries and whole pecans and set aside.

Fold the chopped pecans into the whipped cream and set aside.

Stir the grated chocolate into the pancake batter. Heat 2 teaspoons of oil in a frying pan and drop in tablespoonfuls of the mixture, allowing space for the pancakes to spread a little. Cook them for 2 minutes or until bubbles start to appear on the top, then turn the pancakes over with a palette knife and cook for another 2 minutes.

Continue until you have used all the batter. To serve, make pancake stacks, pour over some chocolate sauce and garnish with whipped cream and strawberries.

Ingredients:

For the batter:

125 g / 4.4 oz plain (all purpose) flour, sifted
1 tbsp cocoa powder, sifted
1 tsp baking powder
2 tsp sugar
pinch of salt
250 ml / 8.7 fl. oz milk
75 g / 2.6 oz dark chocolate, grated
vegetable oil, for frying

For the chocolate sauce:

75 g / 2.6 oz dark chocolate, chopped
125 ml / 4.4 oz double cream
1 tbsp melted butter

To garnish:

80 ml / 2.8 fl. oz maple syrup
300 g / 10.5 oz strawberries, sliced
100 g / 3.5 oz pecan nuts, whole
50 g / 1.8 oz pecan nuts, finely chopped
100 ml / 3.5 fl. oz double cream, whipped

CRÊPES WITH BANANAS AND CHOCOLATE SAUCE

Serves: 4
Prep and cook time: 40 minutes

Ingredients:

For the batter:

125 g / 4.4 oz plain (all purpose) flour, sifted
pinch of salt
2 tsp sugar
1 egg, beaten
250 ml / 8.8 fl. oz milk
2 tbsp vegetable oil, for frying

For the chocolate sauce:

200 g / 7 oz dark chocolate, grated
1 tbsp butter
2 tbsp honey
2 tbsp double cream

To serve:

3 bananas
juice of 1 lemon
icing (confectioners') sugar

Method

Put the flour, salt, sugar, beaten egg and milk into a bowl and beat to make a smooth batter.

Heat a little of the oil in a 20 cm / 8" frying pan and pour in 2 - 3 tablespoons of batter, tilting the pan so it spreads evenly. Cook the crêpe for 1 minute, turn over with a palette knife and cook for another minute or until golden brown. Repeat with the rest of the batter.

Melt the grated chocolate in a bowl over a pan of simmering water. Beat in the butter, honey and cream and remove from the heat.

Slice the bananas and mix with the lemon juice. Cover half of each crêpe with banana slices and chocolate sauce. Fold over the other half, sprinkle with icing sugar and serve.

PANCAKES FOR HALLOWEEN

Makes: 12
Cooking time: 30 minutes

Method

Put the flour into a bowl and add the sugar, beaten egg, melted butter and milk. Beat well to make a smooth batter, then stir in the raisins.

Heat 2 teaspoons of oil in a frying pan and drop on small spoonfuls of the batter, allowing space for the mixture to spread evenly.

Cook the pancakes for 1 minute, then turn them over with a palette knife and cook for another minute, or until golden brown.

Repeat with the rest of the batter, adding more oil as necessary. Stack the pancakes between sheets of kitchen parchment and cover with a clean tea towel to keep them warm until ready to serve.

Ingredients:

125 g / 4.4 oz self-raising flour, sifted
2 tsp sugar
1 egg, beaten
1 tbsp melted butter
150 ml / 5.2 fl. oz milk
100 g / 3.5 oz raisins
vegetable oil, for frying

BEAR FACE PANCAKES

Serves: 4
Prep and cook time: 40 minutes

Ingredients:

For the batter:

125 g / 4.4 oz plain (all purpose) flour, sifted
1 tsp baking powder
pinch of salt
1 tbsp sugar
1 egg, beaten
250 ml / 8.7 fl. oz milk
30 g / 1 oz melted butter
vegetable oil, for frying

To serve:

1 tbsp crème fraiche
12 blueberries
1 strawberry, hulled
4 tbsp maple syrup

Method

Put the flour in a bowl and add the baking powder, salt, sugar, beaten egg, milk and melted butter. Beat well to make a smooth batter. Set the batter aside for 20 minutes.

Heat a little oil in a frying pan. Pour in 2 large spoonfuls of the batter to make the face and 2 teaspoons of batter to make the ears, allowing space for the mixture to spread. Cook for 2 minutes or until bubbles start to rise to the top, then flip the pancake over with a palette knife. Cook for another 2 minutes, or until golden brown.

Carefully remove the bear's face from the pan and put it onto a warm plate. Repeat with the rest of the batter.

Alternatively, you can cut the face shapes from round pancakes once they have cooled.

To serve, pour a tablespoon of maple syrup onto a plate and place the pancake face on top. Decorate with crème fraiche and blueberries for the eyes, a blueberry for the nose and a slice of strawberry for the mouth.

PANCAKES WITH BANANAS AND STRAWBERRIES

Serves: 4
Cooking time: 30 minutes

Method

Put the flour into a bowl, add the other batter ingredients (but not the oil) and beat together until smooth.

Set aside 8 whole strawberries. Put the rest of the strawberries into a blender with the icing sugar and mix together to make a purée. Pass the purée through a sieve and set it aside.

Heat 2 teaspoons of oil in a frying pan and drop in a tablespoon of the pancake batter. Allow it to cook for about 2 minutes or until bubbles start to appear on the top. Flip the pancake over with a palette knife and cook until golden brown.

Repeat with the rest of the batter, adding more oil as needed. Stack the pancakes between sheets of kitchen parchment and cover them with a tea towel to keep them warm.

Slice the bananas and sprinkle with the lemon juice to prevent them from browning. Slice the 8 whole strawberries that you set aside earlier.

Serve the pancakes warm with banana and strawberry slices, strawberry purée and lemon zest.

Ingredients:

For the batter:

250 g / 8.8 oz plain (all purpose) flour, sifted
½ tsp salt
2 tsp sugar
2 tsp baking powder
50 g / 2 tbsp melted butter
300 ml / 10.5 fl. oz milk
2 eggs, beaten
2 tbsp vegetable oil, for frying

For the filling:

400 g / 1 lb strawberries, hulled
1 tbsp icing (confectioners') sugar
3 bananas
1 lemon, juice and zest

INDEX